Jesus Our Salvation

The Person of Jesus Christ in the Salvation of Our Souls

F. Wayne Mac Leod

Light To My Path Book Distribution
Sydney Mines, Nova Scotia Canada B1V 1Y5

Jesus Our Salvation

Copyright © 2022 by F. Wayne Mac Leod

Contents

Preface

We often speak of our salvation as an event in our lives. Some believers can even pinpoint the time and circumstances of the day their lives were changed. As wonderful as that event may have been, I propose that salvation is more about a person than an experience. I would go as far as to say that the Lord Jesus does not just give us salvation; He is our salvation.

To be sure, there were changes in your life. You remember the words spoken by a preacher that day. You can describe the circumstances that led up to the transformation. All too often, however, these events hide what really took place –you met the Lord Jesus.

Without the Lord Jesus, our salvation would not be possible. Remove the person of Christ at any point in this process, and we would be lost without hope. He is the payment for our sin. He is our right standing with the Father. Our strength to live the Christian life is in Him. When we speak of salvation, we refer to the person of the Lord Jesus.

In this study, I want to take the time to consider Jesus Christ as our salvation. My goal is to demonstrate that every aspect of our salvation is found in Him alone.

I trust that what the Lord has been showing me in this matter will be a blessing to each reader. - F. Wayne Mac Leod

Chapter 1 – The Idea of Salvation

Let me begin with the point I want to make in this chapter. The idea of salvation originates in the person of God. Before I was born, God had a plan for my forgiveness and redemption. Listen to the words of the apostle Paul to the Ephesians:

> *(3) Blessed be the God and Father of our Lord Jesus Christ, who has blessed us in Christ with every spiritual blessing in the heavenly places, (4) even as he chose us in him before the foundation of the world, that we should be holy and blameless before him. In love (5) he predestined us for adoption to himself as sons through Jesus Christ, according to the purpose of his will, (6) to the praise of his glorious grace, with which he has blessed us in the Beloved. (7) In him we have redemption through his blood, the forgiveness of our trespasses, according to the riches of his grace, (8) which he lavished upon us, in all wisdom and insight (9) making known to us the mystery of his will, according to his purpose, which he set forth in Christ (10) as a plan for the fullness of time, to unite all things in him, things in heaven and things on earth. - Ephesians 1:3-10 ESV*

I understand that these verses have caused great theological controversy over the years. Consider what the apostle Paul is telling the Ephesians here.

God has blessed us in Christ with every spiritual blessing (verse 4)

Notice here that every spiritual blessing is found in Christ. In other words, there is no spiritual blessing apart from the person of Jesus. The Father has determined that we will only experience the benefits of the Christian life in His Son Jesus.

The plan to bless us in Christ was conceived before the foundation of the world (verse 4)

Notice second that the plan of God to bless us with every spiritual blessing was set out before the foundation of the world. Before the creation of the first man and woman, it was the purpose of God that they would be "holy and blameless before Him" (Ephesians 1:4). He determined that we would be "adopted to himself as sons through Jesus Christ" (verse 5).

From before the foundation of the world, God decided that Jesus Christ would be our connection with Him. He would adopt us "through His blood" (verse 6). Paul reminded the Ephesians that while this was the plan of God from before the foundation of the world, He would reveal this plan in "the fullness of time" (verse 10). The apostle Paul considered it a great privilege to have lived in the days when that plan was revealed through the person of Jesus Christ.

The apostle Peter says something very similar when he writes:

> *(18) knowing that you were ransomed from the futile ways inherited from your forefathers, not with perishable things such as silver or gold, (19) but with the precious blood of Christ, like that of a lamb without blemish or spot. (20) He was foreknown before the foundation of the world but was made manifest in the last times for the sake of you - 1 Peter 1:18-20 ESV*

Peter told his readers that the Lord Jesus was foreknown as a "lamb without blemish or spot," "before the foundation of the world" (verses 19, 20). In other words, even before we were created, God set His Son aside to be a sacrificial lamb for our redemption and forgiveness. All of this took place before the foundations of the earth were laid.

Now let's move ahead in time to Genesis 3. Here we meet Adam, Eve and the serpent who tempted them to eat the forbidden fruit. As we read the story, we watch Satan deceive Eve, causing her to eat from the tree of the knowledge of good and evil. The results were devastating not only for her and her husband but also for their descendants. Sin and death like ugly cancer ravaged the earth. The apostle Paul put it this way:

> *12 Therefore, just as sin came into the world through one man, and death through sin, and so death spread to all men because all sinned— 18 Therefore, as one trespass led to condemnation for all men, so one act of righteousness leads to*

justification and life for all men. 19 For as by the one man's disobedience the many were made sinners, so by the one man's obedience the many will be made righteous. - Romans 5:12, 18-19 ESV

Sin came into the world through Adam. Because of his rebellion, every descendant from that point forward would be born with a sinful nature. Sin, like a deadly disease, bought both spiritual and physical death. It separated us from our Creator and placed us under His judgement.

Notice, however, the words of God to Satan in Genesis 3 just after Adam and Eve fell to the devil's temptation:

15 I will put enmity between you and the woman, and between your offspring and her offspring; he shall bruise your head, and you shall bruise his heel." -Genesis 3:15 ESV

God told Satan of the plan set up in eternity past to redeem the world through the death of His Son Jesus. In the "fullness of time" (Ephesians 1:10), the "lamb without spot or blemish" (1 Peter 1:19) would lay down His life to pay for the sins of His people.

Consider how the apostle John describes Jesus in his gospel:

1 In the beginning was the Word, and the Word was with God, and the Word was God. 2 He was in the beginning with God. 3 All things were made through him, and without him was not any thing made that was made. 4 In him was life, and the life was the light of men. 5 The light shines in

the darkness, and the darkness has not
overcome it. - John 1:1,3-5 ESV

John tells us that Jesus was the Word who existed from the beginning. This Word was the life and the light of men even before the world as we know it was founded. At the right time, He would shine in the darkness of sin, bringing light and life to all who believed in Him.

From the very beginning of time, the purpose of God was that Jesus, His Son, be the source of light and life for His people. He would rescue them from the darkness and death imposed by sin. Way before sin entered the world, Jesus was the solution.

Writing to Timothy, the apostle Paul makes it very clear that the work of salvation was given to Christ Jesus "before the ages began."

> *8 Therefore do not be ashamed of the testimony about our Lord, nor of me his prisoner, but share in suffering for the gospel by the power of God, 9 who saved us and called us to a holy calling, not because of our works but because of his own purpose and grace, which he gave us in Christ Jesus before the ages began, 10 and which now has been manifested through the appearing of our Savior Christ Jesus, who abolished death and brought life and immortality to light through the gospel, - 2 Timothy 1:8-10 ESV*

The apostle told Timothy that we were saved because of the purpose the Father "gave us in Christ Jesus before the ages began" (verse 9).

Way before you or I were born, God had a plan for our salvation. Ages before Satan tempted Eve in the garden, God had a solution. The Lord Jesus was the life and light of the world from the beginning. Even before He created man and woman on the earth, Jesus Christ had been chosen to be the means of our redemption.

It is in this context that the Lord Jesus declared:

> *16 You did not choose me, but I chose you and appointed you that you should go and bear fruit and that your fruit should abide, so that whatever you ask the Father in my name, he may give it to you. - John 15:16 ESV*

The words Jesus speaks here to His disciples apply equally to us all. Our salvation has more to do with Christ's choice than ours. Before I even knew the light of day, God had a plan in place. That plan was revealed in heaven before sin became a reality on earth. Sin did not take God by surprise. Satan has never had the upper hand.

The point I am making in this first chapter is that salvation originates in the mind of God. It was His idea from before the creation of the earth. This salvation would be accomplished through the death of His Son Jesus Christ for us.

There is an incredible mystery to this reality, but there is no denying its truth as taught in the Scriptures. I do not pretend to understand why God placed the tree of the knowledge of good and evil in the garden or why He did not prevent Eve from picking its fruit. I can't give you an answer as to why God allowed Satan into the garden to tempt Adam and Eve. I could speak about free will and choice, but the reality of sin and death remains. What gives me comfort is that God prepared the solution before the problem even existed. God's plan from eternity past has now become my reality.

For Prayer:

Father God, we sometimes read the first few chapters of Genesis as if they were the beginning, but way before the creation of the earth as we know it, You had a plan. Before Eve picked the fruit of the tree of the knowledge of good and evil, You already had a solution in place. Satan did not defeat You in the garden. Jesus, the Lamb of God, had already been set apart to restore Your children to Yourself. From the beginning, Jesus the Word was the life and light that would defeat the death and darkness of sin. Salvation was a choice you made before the foundation of the earth was laid. Thank you, Father, for deciding to redeem us from the fall. Thank you, Lord Jesus, for your decision from eternity past to lay down Your life for me. Thank you, Holy Spirit, for choosing to open my eyes to my need and for giving me life in Christ Jesus.

Chapter 2 – Christ Our Payment

In the first chapter, we saw that salvation originated in the heart of Jesus before the foundation of the earth was laid. Let's move on now to speak about the penalty for sin and rebellion against God. Consider what God told Adam as recorded in Genesis 2:16-17:

> *16 And the LORD God commanded the man, saying, "You may surely eat of every tree of the garden, 17 but of the tree of the knowledge of good and evil you shall not eat, for in the day that you eat of it you shall surely die."- Genesis 2:16-17 ESV*

The Lord told Adam that he would die if he ate from the tree of the knowledge of good and evil. To some, death might seem to be too steep a penalty. Recognize, however, that the Lord God gave this first couple their life and blessed them with every good thing. Every beat of their hearts came from Him. Every breath they took was a privilege He gave. The fruit they ate, and every enjoyment they had, was a gift from His hand. They had nothing without Him. They would perish if He did not sustain them. Should He turn His back, even for a moment, their life would cease.

The God who blessed them was a perfect and holy God who would not tolerate sin and evil. For life and blessing, all God asked was obedience. He warned Adam and Eve that they would die if they chose a path of rebellion. True justice demands punishment in proportion to the crime. What sentence is worthy of the crime of rebelling against Him who gives life and every blessing? What punishment is fair for those who reject the One who sustains and provides their every breath? Is it unjust for God to turn His back on those who refuse to honour Him?

Scripture is very clear about the penalty for sin. Writing to the Romans, the apostle Paul said:

> 23 For the wages of sin is death, but the
> free gift of God is eternal life in Christ
> Jesus our Lord. - Romans 6:23 ESV

Jeremiah the prophet reminded the people of his day about the danger of rebellion against God when he said:

> 30 But everyone shall die for his iniquity.
> Each man who eats sour grapes, his teeth
> shall be set on edge. - Jeremiah 31:30
> ESV

Both Old and New Testaments agree. The penalty for sin is death. We need to understand here that rebellion and the rejection of God is the worst possible sin a person could ever commit. In an age of spiritual apathy, we have often lost sight of this. Scripture reminds us, however, that eternal punishment without hope awaits all who reject the Lord God and His purpose in Christ.

The Lamb of God

In the Old Testament, the Lord established a system of substitutionary sacrifices. When an individual sinned against God, they could bring an animal to the tabernacle and kill it on their behalf. Countless animals died for the sins of God's people. The problem with this system was that while the penalty was paid for each sin, the sinner's heart remained unchanged.

God determined that He would provide a perfect solution to this problem. Listen to the words of John the Baptist about the Lord Jesus in John 1:

> *29 The next day he saw Jesus coming toward him, and said, "Behold, the Lamb of God, who takes away the sin of the world! - John 1:29 ESV*

John refers to Jesus as the "Lamb of God who takes away the sin of the world." The Lord Jesus would become a substitutionary sacrifice for the "sin of the world." He would die as a sacrificial lamb. Like the Old Testament animal sacrifices, Jesus would take my place and pay my penalty. The God who required the sentence of death for sin now lays His own life on the altar to pay my debt in full

Christ's Sacrifice

The Lord Jesus willingly laid down His life to pay the penalty for our sin. The writer to the Hebrews tells us that this single sacrifice of Jesus Christ would never need to be repeated. It was sufficient to cover the sins of all time (past, present and future):

> *12 But when Christ had offered for all time a single sacrifice for sins, he sat down at the right hand of God - Hebrews 10:12 ESV*

Unlike the Old Testament sacrifices that covered only the individual sins of those who offered them, the death of Jesus was also sufficient for the sin of the whole world. Anyone who came to Jesus for forgiveness could find forgiveness:

2 He is the propitiation for our sins, and not for ours only but also for the sins of the whole world. - 1 John 2:2 ESV

Notice also that Jesus' sacrifice will cleanse and make us "holy and blameless and above reproach" before God:

22 he has now reconciled in his body of flesh by his death, in order to present you holy and blameless and above reproach before him, - Colossians 1:22 ESV

This was something that Old Testament sacrifices could never do. Though repeated millions of times, the blood of bulls and goats could not change the human heart. Paul told the Colossians, however, that the death of Christ had as its goal to present them holy and blameless before God.

The apostle Paul told the Romans that Jesus' death justified and gave them right standing with the Father. It saved them from His wrath and restored them to fellowship with God:

8 but God shows his love for us in that while we were still sinners, Christ died for us. 9 Since, therefore, we have now been justified by his blood, much more shall we be saved by him from the wrath of God. 10 For if while we were enemies we were reconciled to God by the death of his Son, much more, now that we are reconciled, shall we be saved by his life. - Romans 5:8-10 ESV

Consider what we have seen here. The penalty for sin and rebellion against God is death. God, however, made a provision for this from the beginning of time. The Lord Jesus Christ would die on my behalf to pay the penalty for my sin and restore me to fellowship. When God told Adam and Eve that death would be the penalty for sin and rebellion, He knew that He would send His Son to take that penalty on Himself.

Here is the point I want to make. When we needed payment for our sin, Jesus did not pull out His cheque book and pay out of the infinite resources of heaven –He was the payment. It is one thing for a millionaire to pay a bill for someone when he has more than enough to do so. It is quite another to sacrifice his life for that person.

Jesus did not just pay our penalty; He was the payment. He did not waive our punishment because He had the right to do so; He "bore our sins in his body:"

> *(24) He himself bore our sins in his body on the tree, that we might die to sin and live to righteousness. By his wounds you have been healed. - 1 Peter 2:24 ESV*

Isaiah prophesied that the Messiah would suffer for our sin when he wrote:

> *(4) Surely, he has borne our griefs and carried our sorrows; yet we esteemed him stricken, smitten by God, and afflicted. (5) But he was pierced for our transgressions; he was crushed for our iniquities; upon him was the chastisement that brought us peace, and with his wounds we are healed. - Isaiah 53:4-5 ESV*

Sin has been the cause of much grief, sorrow, and affliction in this world. Though Jesus did not sin, He experienced its effects in His body. While we long for the day we will be set free from these afflictions, Jesus willingly took them on so that we could be healed. He did not just have compassion on us; He took on our suffering and pain.

Paul went as far as to say that Jesus was actually "made to be sin:"

> *(20) Therefore, we are ambassadors for Christ, God making his appeal through us. We implore you on behalf of Christ, be reconciled to God. (21) For our sake he made him to be sin who knew no sin, so that in him we might become the righteousness of God. - 2 Corinthians 5:20-21 ESV*

Our sin was poured out on Him. He took on those sins and carried them to the cross. The shame of our quilt was placed on His shoulders, and He was lifted up for all to see.

Christ experienced our weaknesses and was tempted in every way just as we are:

> *(15) For we do not have a high priest who is unable to sympathize with our weaknesses, but one who in every respect has been tempted as we are, yet without sin. - Hebrews 4:15 ESV*

The full weight of our suffering, temptations, weakness and grief was piled on Jesus, and the full penalty was declared for Him. He took this on for you and me.

There is a subtle difference between Jesus paying our debt and Jesus being the payment for our debt, but this is a distinction we need to make. Jesus did not just pay for our sins – He was the payment. My debt was not settled by a cheque written on the bank of heaven. Sin required more than a withdrawal from heaven's account. It required nothing less than the death of the Son of God Himself. Jesus paid what no heavenly treasure could. His life alone could pay the debt in full. While the wages of sin is death, the payment for our pardon was nothing less than Jesus Himself. He is the payment for the penalty of sin.

For Prayer:

Lord God, we recognize that You are the source of all life and blessing. Without You, we would surely perish. We confess that though we owe You our obedience and allegiance, we have fallen short. Thank You, Lord Jesus, that You became the sacrificial lamb. You suffered the effects of sin in your body. Though You never sinned, You were the payment for our sin. Thank you for taking the full weight of sin upon Yourself and laying down your life for me. Thank you for being the payment for our sin.

Chapter 3 – Christ Our Forgiveness

We come now to the question of forgiveness and how it relates to the person of Jesus Christ. The point I want to make is that forgiveness is primarily about knowing the Lord Jesus, for apart from knowing Him, there is no true forgiveness. You cannot separate forgiveness from the person of Jesus.

Let me be clear as we begin. As believers, we have all offended a brother or sister and need their pardon. The Lord Jesus commands us to forgive those who offend us (see Matthew 18:21, 22; Luke 17:3). As important as this is, the forgiveness I speak about in this chapter is much greater than this. We may forgive each other for offences done, but how can we receive the forgiveness of God when we cannot even approach Him as sinners?

The forgiveness Jesus offers is exactly this –forgiveness from God. It sets us free from the judgement to come and places us in good standing with the Father. Jesus hinted at this at the celebration of the Passover in Matthew 26 when He said:

> *27 And he took a cup, and when he had given thanks he gave it to them, saying, "Drink of it, all of you, 28 for this is my blood of the covenant, which is poured out for many for the forgiveness of sins. - Matthew 26:27-28 ESV*

Forgiveness through the Blood of Jesus

Notice how Jesus speaks about the blood of the covenant that brought forgiveness of sins. The writer to the Hebrews teaches that forgiveness was only possible through the shedding of blood:

> *(22) Indeed, under the law almost everything is purified with blood, and without the shedding of blood there is no forgiveness of sins. - Hebrews 9:22 ESV*

This immediately separates the type of forgiveness Jesus offers from what we offer a brother or sister. None of us had to die to be forgiven.

Jesus told His disciples in Matthew 26:28 that it was His blood that would bring the required pardon. Only the blood of the sinless Lamb of God could set us free from the penalty of sin and restore us to a right standing with God. Forgiveness, therefore, is through the shed blood of the Lord Jesus Christ on the cross.

The apostle Paul understood when he wrote:

> *7 In him we have redemption through his blood, the forgiveness of our trespasses, according to the riches of his grace - Ephesians 1:7 ESV*

According to Paul, redemption and forgiveness of trespasses are through the blood of Jesus Christ shed for us on the cross of Calvary. His death brings us forgiveness, for it pays the penalty for our sins in full. The only blood that can bring this kind of forgiveness is the untainted blood of the spotless Lamb of God. No other blood would do. True forgiveness is through the blood of Jesus alone.

Forgiveness in the Name of Jesus

Not only is forgiveness through the blood of Jesus, but It is extended to us in His name. Listen to what Peter proclaimed in Jerusalem during Pentecost:

> *38 And Peter said to them, "Repent and be baptized every one of you in the name of Jesus Christ for the forgiveness of your sins, and you will receive the gift of the Holy Spirit. - Acts 2:38 ESV*

Peter challenged those who listened to him to seek forgiveness in the name of the Lord Jesus Christ. When asked to defend this teaching before the rulers, Peter boldly proclaimed that there was salvation in no other name:

> *12 And there is salvation in no one else, for there is no other name under heaven given among men by which we must be saved."- Acts 4:12 ESV*

The Lord Jesus reminded His disciples that they were to proclaim forgiveness of sin to the nations in His name alone:

> *(46) and said to them, "Thus it is written, that the Christ should suffer*

and on the third day rise from the dead,
(47) and that repentance for the
forgiveness of sins should be
proclaimed in his name to all nations,
beginning from Jerusalem. - Luke
24:46-47 ESV

According to Peter in Acts 10:43, the Old Testament prophets proclaimed that forgiveness would come through the name of this coming Messiah:

43   To him all the prophets bear
witness that everyone who believes in
him receives forgiveness of sins
through his name."- Acts 10:43 ESV

Isaiah prophesied that God would lay a precious and tested cornerstone in Zion as a sure foundation. The prophet went on to say that those who believed in that stone would "not be in haste." The picture here is one of an enemy's sudden attack. When the alarm sounded, the people of the city would hurriedly gather their belongings and flee. Those who believed in the stone laid in Zion, however, would have no fear. Isaiah went on to say that their "covenant with death would be annulled," and their agreement with Sheol, the grave, would not stand. Those who trusted this Rock in Zion would not be overwhelmed (Isaiah 28:16-18):

(16) therefore thus says the Lord GOD,
"Behold, I am the one who has laid as a
foundation in Zion, a stone, a tested
stone, a precious cornerstone, of a sure
foundation: 'Whoever believes will not
be in haste.' (17) And I will make justice
the line, and righteousness the plumb

line; and hail will sweep away the
refuge of lies, and waters will
overwhelm the shelter." (18) Then your
covenant with death will be annulled,
and your agreement with Sheol will not
stand; when the overwhelming scourge
passes through, you will be beaten
down by it. - Isaiah 28:16-18 ESV

The stone in Zion was the Lord Jesus. He would extend forgiveness and pardon to all who believed in Him. When the judgement came, those who believed in Him would not be put to shame. These words were proclaimed many years before the Lord Jesus came to this earth.

The psalmist used a similar illustration in Psalm 118 when he said:

(21) I thank you that you have
answered me and have become my
salvation. (22) The stone that the
builders rejected has become the
cornerstone. - Psalms 118:21-22 ESV

The psalmist speaks about how Jesus the stone was rejected but saved of all who trusted in Him. In the psalmist's mind, salvation and forgiveness of sin were found only in the Rock of Zion. Old Testament believers looked forward to the Messiah who would come to offer forgiveness through His name. Scripture makes it quite clear that there is only forgiveness in the name of Jesus. That is to say, in the person of Jesus Christ alone can we experience pardon and right standing with God.

The Authority to Forgive

In Mark 2, we have the story of the healing of a man with paralysis. The scribes were present that day when Jesus healed him. A disagreement began when Jesus made the following declaration:

> *(5) And when Jesus saw their faith, he said to the paralytic, "Son, your sins are forgiven." - Mark 2:5 ESV*

Upon hearing these words, the scribes accused Jesus of blasphemy, stating that only God could forgive sin:

> *(6) Now some of the scribes were sitting there, questioning in their hearts, (7) "Why does this man speak like that? He is blaspheming! Who can forgive sins but God alone?" - Mark 2:6-7 ESV*

Jesus knew their thoughts and declared:

> *(8) "Why do you question these things in your hearts? (9) Which is easier, to say to the paralytic, 'Your sins are forgiven,' or to say, 'Rise, take up your bed and walk'? (10) But that you may know that the Son of Man has authority on earth to forgive sins"—he said to the paralytic— (11) "I say to you, rise, pick up your bed, and go home." - Mark 2:8-11 ESV*

The paralytic immediately picked up his bed and walked (Mark 2:12). Note the words of Jesus in verse 9: *"But that you may know that the Son of Man has authority on earth to forgive sins."* The paralytic was healed to prove this point. The father has given the power of forgiveness to His Son, Jesus Christ. This is also the clear teaching of Peter in Acts 5:31 where, speaking of Jesus, he said:

> *31 God exalted him at his right hand as Leader and Savior, to give repentance to Israel and forgiveness of sins. - Acts 5:31 ESV*

The Father has exalted Jesus and given Jesus the power to give repentance and forgiveness. No one else has this authority. If you want to be forgiven, there is only one person who has the authority to forgive you – the Lord Jesus. Every one of us must come to Him if we want this pardon. There is no forgiveness apart from Him. According to Jesus, the Father has passed all judgement to Him:

> *(22) For the Father judges no one, but has given all judgment to the Son, - John 5:22 ESV*

The wonderful news is that we have the promise of Jesus, the sole administrator of forgiveness, that if we confess our sins, He will forgive us:

> *9 If we confess our sins, he is faithful and just to forgive us our sins and to cleanse us from all unrighteousness. - 1 John 1:9 ESV*

What does all this teach us? To know forgiveness, we must know Jesus. Forgiveness is through His blood and in His name alone. He is the only one who has the authority of the Father to proclaim our pardon and forgiveness. All who want to know this pardon must stand before Him.   We cannot separate forgiveness from the person of Jesus Christ –He is our forgiveness. His blood brings our forgiveness, and He alone has been given the right to declare our pardon. Only in His name and by his authority can any true forgiveness be offered.

Forgiveness is not just something that happens to us. It is so connected with the person of Jesus Cheiar that ultimately, He is our forgiveness. Without Jesus, there is no forgiveness. Apart from His blood, there is no pardon. His declaration alone will set us free from guilt.   Our complete and total pardon rests in the person of the Lord Jesus Christ, what He has done and what he declares to us personally. If you want to be forgiven, you need to know Jesus.

For Prayer:

Lord Jesus, thank you that there is forgiveness through your work on the cross of Calvary. I confess that there is no other way for me to have peace with the Father but through You. I recognize that there is no other name by which I can be saved but Yours. I believe that You alone have been given the authority to pardon sin. If I am to be forgiven, I must stand before You alone. All judgement has been given to You. I stand before You now and ask for pardon and forgiveness of sin. I confess that I am unworthy of this but know You to be a God of grace and mercy.   I confess You to be my only guarantee and assurance of forgiveness. My pardon is so tied up in You and Your work that You are my pardon –I trust in nothing but You and rest confident in Your promise alone.

Chapter 4 – Jesus the Way

How would you respond if I asked you: "What is the way to your house?" You would likely give me a set of directions. You would tell me what street to follow, where to turn, and your house number. What if I asked you: "What is the way to heaven?" How would you respond? I suppose some would tell me that I needed to be good to my neighbours, go to church every Sunday and live a certain way. But how would Jesus answer this question? Listen to His response in John 14:6:

> *6 Jesus said to him, "I am the way, and*
> *the truth, and the life. No one comes to*
> *the Father except through me. - John 14:6*
> *ESV*

You can't get into a spaceship and travel to a place called heaven by following a certain set of coordinates. You can't even get there by following a certain set of rules or by living an especially good life. Jesus tells us that He is the way and that no one can come to the Father apart from Him. The way to heaven is a person –the Lord Jesus. Apart from Jesus, there is no way we can get there.

About ten minutes from where I live is a passenger ferry that takes cars and trucks to an island province about six hours away. If you were to ask me the way to this province, I would tell you that the ferry is the way. If you want to go there, you need to drive your car onto that boat and let it take you all the way. Jesus told His listeners something similar when He told them that He was the way to the Father. If they were going to get to heaven, they needed to trust Him to do it for them. He was the only one who could get them there. To know Jesus is to know the way.

If I get lost while travelling, I might stop a person on the street and ask for directions. However, this is not what Jesus is telling us when He teaches that He is the way. He is not telling us that He knows the way, and if we come to Him, He can show us how to get there on our own. Jesus is very clear when He says: "I am the way."

If I want to find heaven, I must first find Jesus. The Father will only allow those who know His Son to enter. This is the clear teaching of Jesus in the passage quoted above:

> *No one comes to the Father except through me. - John 14:6 ESV*

In John 10, the Lord Jesus told a parable about a sheepfold where He describes Himself as the only entrance:

> *[7] So Jesus again said to them, "Truly, truly, I say to you, I am the door of the sheep. [8] All who came before me are thieves and robbers, but the sheep did not listen to them. [9] I am the door. If anyone enters by me, he will be saved and will go in and out and find pasture. – John 10:7-9 ESV*

There is only one doorway into heaven, and Jesus tells us that He is that doorway. If you want to go to heaven, you must pass through Him.

As a sinner, I cannot enter until the penalty for sin has been paid. Where do I go to have this addressed? I must go to Jesus. As one who has offended God, I must first be made right with Him to be with Him forever. How can I be made right with God? I need forgiveness and pardon. This, too, comes from Jesus. Everything we need for heaven is found in the person of the Lord Jesus and nobody else. His death paid my penalty. His declaration sets me free from guilt and condemnation.

One sacrifice after another was made for sin throughout the Old Testament, but the wall between God and human beings remained. This was pictured most graphically in the tabernacle where a curtain separated the people of God from the Most Holy Place, where God revealed His presence. No matter how many sacrifices were made, that curtain of separation remained. Writing about this, the author of Hebrews says:

> *8 By this the Holy Spirit indicates that the way into the holy places is not yet opened as long as the first section is still standing ... 11 But when Christ appeared as a high priest of the good things that have come, then through the greater and more perfect tent (not made with hands, that is, not of this creation) 12 he entered once for all into the holy places, not by means of the blood of goats and calves but by means of his own blood, thus securing an eternal redemption. - Hebrews 9:8,11-12 ESV*

"When Christ appeared as a high priest," everything changed – He secured "an eternal redemption." In other words, the sacrifice of Jesus Christ opened the door for us to enter the presence of the Father. Listen to t what happened when Jesus died on the cross:

> *(50) And Jesus cried out again with a loud voice and yielded up his spirit. (51) And behold, the curtain of the temple was torn in two, from top to bottom. And the earth shook, and the rocks were split. (52) The tombs also were opened. And many bodies of the saints who had fallen asleep were raised, (53) and coming out of the tombs after his resurrection they went into the holy city and appeared to many. - Matthew 27:50-53 ESV*

Every barrier to fellowship with the Father was broken when the Lord Jesus died. He became the bridge between sinful human beings and God. We now have access to the Father through Him:

18 For through him we both have access in one Spirit to the Father. - Ephesians 2:18 ESV

The writer to the Hebrews tells us that we can now enter the Most Holy place into the presence of the Father with confidence because of Christ's blood shed for us:

> *19 Therefore, brothers, since we have confidence to enter the holy places by the blood of Jesus, - Hebrews 10:19 ESV*

The apostle Paul repeated the same thought when he told the Ephesians that in Christ, we have boldness and confidence to access that Father:

*12 in whom we have boldness and access
with confidence through our faith in him. -
Ephesians 3:12 ESV*

We have already examined the words of Jesus in John 10 when He said:

*7 "Truly, truly, I say to you, I am the door
of the sheep... 9 I am the door. If anyone
enters by me, he will be saved and will go
in and out and find pasture. - John 10:7, 9
ESV*

In New Testament times, a shepherd would gather his sheep into a fold and then stand at the entrance guarding them. Nothing could come in or out of the single opening unless it passed through the shepherd. He became the door to the sheepfold. Jesus tells us that you need to find Him to enter the fold. In fact, He is the door into the fold. This was the teaching of the apostle Paul when he wrote to the Romans in chapter 5 of his epistle:

*1 Therefore, since we have been justified
by faith, we have peace with God through
our Lord Jesus Christ. 2 Through him we
have also obtained access by faith into
this grace in which we stand, and we
rejoice in hope of the glory of God. -
Romans 5:1-2 ESV*

According to Paul, we have access through the Lord Jesus as the doorway to forgiveness and eternal life. Jesus doesn't just know the way; He is the way. The way to heaven and eternal life is a person. It is not a set of directions to follow or a way of living. The way to God is Jesus. If you want heaven,

35

you need Jesus. If you want access to the Father, you must go through Jesus the door.

Salvation is not a set of directions we follow to find heaven. Nor is it a lifestyle we choose to gain the approval of God. The way to God is a person. We do injustice to the person of Jesus Christ when we reduce salvation to a set of doctrines or practices. The way to God is firmly rooted in the person of His Son. Doctrines or religious practices will not save us; only the person of Jesus can do that. To know the way to God, you must know the person of Jesus.

For Prayer:

Lord God, forgive us for reducing salvation to a set of doctrines and lifestyles. We confess that our beliefs will never save us, nor will our good life. We recognize that Satan believes in Jesus, but he will be condemned forever. Help us keep our focus on the person of the Lord Jesus, who alone is the way to God. He is the door through which we must pass. He is the one upon whom we must rely to access the Father. To know salvation, we must know the person of Jesus.

Chapter 5 – Jesus the Truth

In John 18, we have the record of a conversation between the Lord Jesus and Pilate. Pilate asked Jesus whether he was a king. Jesus told him He was, but His kingdom was not of this world. He went on to tell Pilate that He had come to bear witness to the truth. Pilate responded with words that have echoed throughout the generations: "What is truth?" - John 18:38, ESV.

In our day, truth is subjective. My truth is not someone else's. In a post-truth era, we make up our reality. Biological facts no longer matter when it comes to determining the sex of an individual. There is a rebellion against any authority determining right or wrong behaviour. Law enforcement officers are seen as enemies. Opinion-based news reports have taken the place of objective reporting. Truth is what I want it to be; facts get in the way.

For those of us seeking to find the answer, the question remains: what is truth? How did the Lord Jesus answer this question? He leaves no doubt about what He believed and taught when He said:

> *(6) "I am the way, and the truth, and the life. No one comes to the Father except through me. - John 14:6 ESV*

Jesus made a bold declaration. He told all who would listen to Him that He was the truth. The truth Jesus speaks about here relates to the meaning and purpose of life. Jesus is the reason to live. He is also its goal and purpose.

The apostle John introduced Jesus in his gospel with the following words:

> *(1) In the beginning was the Word, and the Word was with God, and the Word was God. (2) He was in the beginning with God. (3) All things were made through him, and without him was not any thing made that was made. (4) In him was life, and the life was the light of men. (5) The light shines in the darkness, and the darkness has not overcome it. (6) There was a man sent from God, whose name was John (7) He came as a witness, to bear witness about the light, that all might believe through him. (8) He was not the light, but came to bear witness about the light. (9) The true light, which gives light to everyone, was coming into the world. - John 1:1-9 ESV*

John tells us that Jesus, as the Word, was in the beginning with God (verses 1-2). That Word made all things (verse 3). In Him was the "light of men" (verse 4). The light in Him was "the true light" that gives light to everyone coming into the world (verse 9).

Consider the title given to Jesus here. He is the Word. The term does not refer to the sound coming from the mouth but the wisdom and intellect of God. In other words, Jesus was the expression of the truth of God. He perfectly demonstrated the truth in His life, actions and teaching. If you want to know the truth about God and His purpose, you need to look to

Jesus. He is the ultimate demonstration and expression of that truth.

John goes on in verse 14 to say more about this Word:

> *(14) And the Word became flesh and dwelt among us, and we have seen his glory, glory as of the only Son from the Father, full of grace and truth. - John 1:14 ESV*

Jesus the Word became flesh. The intellect and wisdom of God were demonstrated in the person of Jesus, who became a man. John tells us that the man Jesus was "full of grace and truth." To know the truth, we must look to Him. The apostle made it clear that the truth of God and His purpose come to us in the person of the Lord Jesus:

> *(17) For the law was given through Moses; grace and truth came through Jesus Christ. - John 1:17 ESV*

Jesus is the source of all truth about God and His purpose for us in this world. His life not only demonstrates the truth of God, He is the truth.

Consider also the words of Jesus to the Jews in John 8:31:

> *(31) So Jesus said to the Jews who had believed him, "If you abide in my word, you are truly my disciples, (32) and you will know the truth, and the truth will set you free." - John 8:31-32 ESV*

Jesus speaks here to Jews who believed in Him. He told them that if they remained in His word, they would know the truth, and that truth would set them free. Consider this for a moment. What is the truth that sets us free? I have met people who believe that Jesus is the Son of God, but they have not experienced the salvation that sets them free from judgement. The truth spoken of here is not just a set of doctrines to believe. It is much deeper than this. Jesus is the truth. It is Him who sets us free. You can understand all the Bible says about Jesus, but if you do not come to Him, You will never experience freedom. Jesus is the truth that sets us free. John explains this more fully when he says:

> *(3) And this is eternal life, that they know you, the only true God, and Jesus Christ whom you have sent. - John 17:3 ESV*

To experience eternal life, we must know the true God and His Son Jesus Christ.

Listen to the words of John about Jesus in his first epistle:

> *(20) And we know that the Son of God has come and has given us understanding, so that we may know him who is true; and we are in him who is true, in his Son Jesus Christ. He is the true God and eternal life. - 1 John 5:20 ESV*

John describes Jesus as the true God who has come to give us understanding. In other words, Jesus came so we could know the true God and His plan for eternal life.

In Revelation 3:14, Jesus describes Himself as the "faithful and true witness, the beginning of God's creation:"

> *(14) "And to the angel of the church in Laodicea write: 'The words of the Amen, the faithful and true witness, the beginning of God's creation. - Revelation 3:14 ESV*

His life is a perfect demonstration of the truth of God for us. He embodies the purpose and will of God for His creation.

Consider the words of John as recorded in Revelation 19:11:

> *(11) Then I saw heaven opened, and behold, a white horse! The one sitting on it is called Faithful and True, and in righteousness he judges and makes war. (12) His eyes are like a flame of fire, and on his head are many diadems, and he has a name written that no one knows but himself. (13) He is clothed in a robe dipped in blood, and the name by which he is called is The Word of God. - Revelation 19:11-13 ESV*

In his vision, the apostle John saw a rider on a white horse. The name of this rider was Faithful and True. He came to exercise judgement on the earth and was clothed in a robe dipped in blood. John identifies him as "The Word of God" in verse 13. The Lord Jesus, as the Word of God, bears the name Faithful and True. This was not just a name but a reflection of His person. He was the Faithful and True witness of Revelation 3:14.

It is easy to see truth as a set of beliefs and doctrines. Truth is more than this, however. It is embodied in the person of Jesus Christ. It is so rooted in Him that you must first know Jesus to know the truth. You cannot separate Jesus from the truth, nor can you find truth apart from Jesus. To know Jesus is to see the truth.

For Prayer:

Lord Jesus, we recognize that You are the truth of God, perfectly demonstrated in human form. You came as the Word to give us understanding and knowledge of the purpose of the Father. Thank you that You opened our eyes to see You as the truth. Forgive us for how we have so often separated truth from the person of Jesus and reduced it to a set of doctrines. We confess that until we find You, these doctrines and beliefs will never save us. Give us the passion of Paul, who said: "For I decided to know nothing among you except Jesus Christ and him crucified" (1 Corinthians 2:2 ESV). We know that to know Christ is to know the truth.

Chapter 6 – Jesus our Life

In the last chapter, we examined the words of Jesus, who said:

> *(6) "I am the way, and the truth, and the life. No one comes to the Father except through me. - John 14:6 ESV*

We have already seen how Jesus is the way and the truth. Let's take a moment here to examine the final claim of Jesus in this verse.

I want to begin with John 1:1-4:

> *(1) In the beginning was the Word, and the Word was with God, and the Word was God. (2) He was in the beginning with God. (3) All things were made through him, and without him was not any thing made that was made. (4) In him was life, and the life was the light of men. - John 1:1-4 ESV*

John begins his gospel by introducing Jesus as the Word. We considered this in the last chapter. Notice what John tells us about Jesus the Word. He was with God in the beginning, and all things were made through Him. Jesus was one with the Father and the Spirit in creating the world. We owe our existence to the Lord Jesus as our Creator. Our life comes from Him.

Notice also in verse 4 that John tells us that in Jesus was life and that this life was our light. In other words, we only see the light of life because of the grace of God through Jesus. We must understand here that while Jesus was involved in creation with the Father and the Spirit, this physical life is not the only life we have because of Jesus. Consider the words of the apostle Paul to the Ephesians:

(4) But God, being rich in mercy, because
of the great love with which he loved us,
(5) even when we were dead in our
trespasses, made us alive together with
Christ— by grace you have been saved—
- Ephesians 2:4-5 ESV

Paul told the Ephesians that they were spiritually dead and had no relationship with God because of sin. In His infinite mercy, the Lord God made them "alive together with Christ." In other words, through the work of His Son, the Lord God gave spiritual life to those who were separated from Him.

The apostle shared this thought with the Colossians when he wrote:

(13) And you, who were dead in your
trespasses and the uncircumcision of your
flesh, God made alive together with him,
having forgiven us all our trespasses -
Colossians 2:13 ESV

Those who were dead to God, and separated eternally from Him, were made alive "together" with Christ through the forgiveness of sin.

Notice how the apostle uses "together with Christ" and "together with Him" in these two verses. The word together is important. It implies that the spiritual life we have is intimately connected to Christ and that we would not have life apart from Him. You cannot separate the person of Jesus Christ from this new life. Jesus tells us in John 14:6, quoted above that He is the life we receive.

Listen to what Jesus told those who questioned His authority in John 5:

> *(21) For as the Father raises the dead and gives them life, so also the Son gives life to whom he will - John 5:21 ESV*

Jesus has the power of life in Himself. He is the source of both physical and spiritual life. Not only is Jesus the source of life, but he also sustains this life as we trust in Him. He declares Himself to be the Bread of Life in John 6:35:

> *(35) Jesus said to them, "I am the bread of life; whoever comes to me shall not hunger, and whoever believes in me shall never thirst. - John 6:35 ESV*

If we don't eat, we will perish. We need food to sustain our lives. Jesus tells us here that not only does he give life, but as the Bread of life, He also maintains it. This is true for both our physical and spiritual lives.

The focus of this study relates to Jesus our salvation. Through the work of the Lord Jesus on the cross of Calvary, we are not only pardoned but received new life. Writing to the Corinthians, the apostle Paul said:

> *(17) Therefore, if anyone is in Christ, he is a new creation. The old has passed away; behold, the new has come. - 2 Corinthians 5:17 ESV*

What is this new life we receive? Jesus answers this for us in John 11:25 when He said:

> *(25) Jesus said to her, "I am the resurrection and the life. Whoever believes in me, though he die, yet shall he live, - John 11:25 ESV*

Speaking to Martha that day, Jesus told her that He was the life and that whoever believed in Him would not die. The new life we experience is Jesus in us.

In John 6:57, Jesus told His listeners that if they wanted to know life, they needed to feed on Him:

> *(57) As the living Father sent me, and I live because of the Father, so whoever feeds on me, he also will live because of me. - John 6:57 ESV*

If we want life, there is only one place we can go to find it – the person of the Lord Jesus. We must draw this life from Him and depend on Him for it. Peter boldly told the Jews of his day that they killed the author of life when they crucified the Lord Jesus:

> *(15) and you killed the Author of life, whom God raised from the dead. To this we are witnesses. - Acts 3:15 ESV*

What is important for us to understand is that Jesus is much more than the author of life for us. He is our life. We cannot separate the life we have in Christ from the person of Christ. Writing to the Colossians, the apostle Paul said:

(4) When Christ who is your life appears,
then you also will appear with him in glory.
- Colossians 3:4 ESV

Do you see what the apostle said here? Christ is our life. He does not tell us that Christ gave us life, although that is also true. Paul specifically tells us that the life in us is Christ. The new life we know is the very presence of the Lord Jesus in us.

The apostle puts it in another way when he wrote to the Galatians:

(20) I have been crucified with Christ. It is no longer I who live, but Christ who lives in me. And the life I now live in the flesh I live by faith in the Son of God, who loved me and gave himself for me. - Galatians 2:20 ESV

The very spirit of Christ dwelled in the person of the apostle Paul. The life he experienced was the life of Christ being manifested in Him. The life Paul experienced was not some impersonal force but the reL presence of Jesus.

Writing to Timothy, the apostle said:

(1) Paul, an apostle of Christ Jesus by the will of God according to the promise of the life that is in Christ Jesus. - 2 Timothy 1:1 ESV

The life Paul experienced was in the person of Christ Jesus. This was what the apostle John told his readers in 1 John 5:11-12:

(11) And this is the testimony, that God gave us eternal life, and this life is in his Son. (12) Whoever has the Son has life;

whoever does not have the Son of God
does not have life. - 1 John 5:11-12 ESV

If you have Jesus, you have life. Jesus is the life in us. His presence in us is our life.

The apostle Paul was very much aware of this presence of the Lord Jesus in him as he walked in his calling. In fact, he was so aware of Christ's presence in him that he refused to take credit for what Christ had accomplished in Him.

> *(18) For I will not venture to speak of anything except what Christ has accomplished through me to bring the Gentiles to obedience—by word and deed, - Romans 15:18 ESV*

Paul reminded the Corinthians that God had shone the light of the glory of Christ in their hearts as well:

> *(6) For God, who said, "Let light shine out of darkness," has shone in our hearts to give the light of the knowledge of the glory of God in the face of Jesus Christ. – 2 Corinthians 4:6 ESV*

Those who know the Lord Jesus have His light shining in their heart. This light is not separate from Christ but the very light of His presence in them.

Paul compared himself to a simple jar of clay holding a priceless treasure –the glory of Christ:

> *(7) But we have this treasure in jars of clay, to show that the surpassing power belongs to God and not to us. – 2 Corinthians 4:7 ESV*

The surpassing power of Christ dwelt in Paul. As a result, He did what was impossible in his human strength. Those who saw his works knew that the power in Him was the very power of Christ. The apostle went on to describe the life of the believer when he said:

> *(10) always carrying in the body the death of Jesus, so that the life of Jesus may also be manifested in our bodies. (11) For we who live are always being given over to death for Jesus' sake, so that the life of Jesus also may be manifested in our mortal flesh. - 2 Corinthians 4:6-7,10-11 ESV*

Notice how Paul told the Corinthians that the life of Jesus was manifested in his mortal flesh. The life Paul experienced was the life of Jesus in him. It was the power of Jesus that enabled him. It was the glory of Christ that shone from his heart.

It is easy for us to believe that Jesus gives us life as an impersonal force. This was not how Paul saw the life He received. The life Jesus gives is His own. He gave this life on the cross, and He gives Himself to all who believe. Jesus is the life and power you experience. He does not leave you to yourself but chooses to live and work in You.

When I see the life in me as the person of Christ, I surrender to Him and His leading. I find myself overwhelmed by the reality of His presence. I step out boldly in obedience and experience the power of His Spirit. I realize that when great things happen, it is not my strength that accomplished it but the very person of Christ through me and in this, I bow in praise and thanksgiving.

For Prayer:

Lord Jesus, thank you for my physical life. I recognize that it has come from You. I acknowledge that you have sustained and protected me from my birth. Thank you that I know Your presence in my mortal flesh. Thank you for the evidence I see of this in my life as you change me day by day into Your image. I praise You for the power that You have made available to me through Your presence in my life –power to overcome and power to serve. I recognize that you dwell in a fragile "jar of clay," but I pray that I demonstrate Your presence in me to the world. May Your presence and power be evident for all to see, and may I willingly take a back seat so that all will see You.

Chapter 7 – Christ Our Righteousness

Righteousness has to do with being in right standing with God. The enemy to righteousness is sin. Sin separates us from a holy God and places us under His judgement. As a just God, He must punish us. As a holy God, He must separate Himself from the sinner. The problem is that we all fall short of God's standard. Quoting from Psalm 14, the apostle Paul says:

> *(10) as it is written: "None is righteous, no, not one; (11) no one understands; no one seeks for God. (12) All have turned aside; together they have become worthless; no one does good, not even one." - Romans 3:10-12 ESV*

Romans 6:23 tells us that the "wages of sin is death." This death is physical and spiritual in nature and implies an eternal separation from God. How is right standing with God possible when we are sinners by nature? The answer comes in the person of Jesus Christ. Listen once again to the words of the apostle Paul in Romans 5:

> *(6) For while we were still weak, at the right time Christ died for the ungodly. (7) For one will scarcely die for a righteous person—though perhaps for a good person one would dare even to die— (8) but God shows his love for us in that while we were still sinners, Christ died for us.*

*(9) Since, therefore, we have now been
justified by his blood, much more shall we
be saved by him from the wrath of God.
(10) For if while we were enemies we were
reconciled to God by the death of his Son,
much more, now that we are reconciled,
shall we be saved by his life. (11) More
than that, we also rejoice in God through
our Lord Jesus Christ, through whom we
have now received reconciliation. -
Romans 5:6-11 ESV*

The Lord Jesus took sin's penalty and "died for us" (verse 8). His death paid our sentence in full and reconciled us to God. With our debt paid, we can now be in a right relationship with God.

While we acknowledge that the Lord Jesus paid for our sin on the cross, the problem is that we still sin. In Matthew 5:20, the Lord Jesus, speaking about the scribes and the Pharisees, said:

*(20) For I tell you, unless your
righteousness exceeds that of the scribes
and Pharisees, you will never enter the
kingdom of heaven. - Matthew 5:20 ESV*

There were none so religious as the scribes and Pharisees in Israel. They were careful to observe the law of Moses in every detail. People looked up to them as an example of what it meant to be righteous. Jesus, however, told His listeners that the righteousness God expected was greater than that which the Pharisees and scribes demonstrated. Jesus went on in that same discussion to say:

Christ Our Righteousness

(48) You therefore must be perfect, as your heavenly Father is perfect. - Matthew 5:48 ESV

God's standard of righteousness is perfection. Anything less than this is unacceptable to Him. Only perfection can enter His presence —such is the absolute holiness of God. The problem is that while the Lord Jesus has forgiven us, we are far from perfect and still fall short of His standard in our actions, thoughts and attitudes. How can we be right with God when we still sin?

Consider the words of Paul in Romans 1:

(17) For in it the righteousness of God is revealed from faith for faith, as it is written, "The righteous shall live by faith." - Romans 1:17 ESV

The apostle spoke about righteousness from God revealed and lived out in faith. Notice two details here. First, the righteousness Paul talks about is not our righteousness but the "righteousness of God." Second, those who experience this right standing with God do so by faith.

Paul explains what he means more fully in Romans 3 when he says:

(21) But now the righteousness of God has been manifested apart from the law, although the Law and the Prophets bear witness to it— (22) the righteousness of God through faith in Jesus Christ for all who believe. For there is no distinction: - Romans 3:21-22 ESV

The righteousness Paul speaks about here is "apart from the law." In other words, it is not based on our ability to obey God's law. For thousands of years, the people of God attempted to follow this law but failed. No one could meet its standard. According to Paul, however, God now reveals a righteousness that has nothing to do with how well we can live the Christian life. This righteousness, the apostle tells us, comes through faith in the Lord Jesus.

Paul describes this righteousness as a "free gift" in Romans 5:

> *(17) For if, because of one man's trespass, death reigned through that one man, much more will those who receive the abundance of grace and the free gift of righteousness reign in life through the one man Jesus Christ. (18) Therefore, as one trespass led to condemnation for all men, so one act of righteousness leads to justification and life for all men. - Romans 5:17-18 ESV*

Paul tells us about a righteous right standing with God that comes to us as a "free gift." This gift of righteousness does not depend on how good we are. It is based solely on the work of the "one man Jesus Christ" and His "one act of righteousness." That act of righteousness was His death on the cross that paid our sins in full.

To understand this more fully, consider what Paul tells us in Romans 8:6-11:

> *(8) Those who are in the flesh cannot please God. (9) You, however, are not in the flesh but in the Spirit, if in fact the Spirit*

*of God dwells in you. Anyone who does
not have the Spirit of Christ does not
belong to him. (10) But if Christ is in you,
although the body is dead because of sin,
the Spirit is life because of righteousness.
(11) If the Spirit of him who raised Jesus
from the dead dwells in you, he who raised
Christ Jesus from the dead will also give
life to your mortal bodies through his Spirit
who dwells in you.- Romans 8:8-11 ESV*

The apostle told the Romans that "the flesh cannot please God." This body with its natural impulses must die. It will not enter the presence of God, nor can it because it is sinful. Paul tells us, however, that we "are not in the flesh but in the Spirit." Those who know the Lord Jesus have been born again. Jesus told Nicodemus that unless he experienced this new birth, he would not see the kingdom of God:

*(3) Jesus answered him, "Truly, truly, I say
to you, unless one is born again he cannot
see the kingdom of God." - John 3:3 ESV*

Paul considered his fleshly nature dead. While in his earthly body, the apostle still experienced its lusts and sinful desires, but he did not identify with them. He spoke of this in Romans 7 when he said:

*(21) So I find it to be a law that when I
want to do right, evil lies close at hand.
(22) For I delight in the law of God, in my
inner being, (23) but I see in my members
another law waging war against the law of
my mind and making me captive to the law
of sin that dwells in my members. (24)
Wretched man that I am! Who will deliver*

me from this body of death? (25) Thanks
be to God through Jesus Christ our Lord!
So then, I myself serve the law of God with
my mind, but with my flesh I serve the law
of sin. - Romans 7:21-25 ESV

Do you see the struggle here? Paul delighted in the law of God, but his flesh and sinful mind waged war against that law. He lived with what he called a body of death. That body of death was his sinful flesh that had been condemned to die. He carried this around like a dead horse on his back, but it was not who he was anymore. He longed to be free of this body so He could walk in deep and intimate fellowship with God.

It is important to understand that the apostle did not define himself by his flesh but by the new life He had received from Christ. Notice what he said in verse 22: "I delight in the law of God, in my inner being." Paul received this inner being when he was born again. There was a day when he placed that old fleshly nature on the cross and died to it. Paul became a new person that day. He spoke of this to the Corinthians when he said:

(17) Therefore, if anyone is in Christ, he is
a new creation. The old has passed away;
behold, the new has come. - 2
Corinthians 5:17 ESV

Paul considered his old fleshly nature dead. He chose to live now in the new life He had received from God through faith in the work of Jesus Christ. Notice what Paul told the Galatians about this new life:

(20) I have been crucified with Christ. It is
no longer I who live, but Christ who lives in

me. And the life I now live in the flesh I
live by faith in the Son of God, who loved
me and gave himself for me. (21) I do not
nullify the grace of God, for if
righteousness were through the law, then
Christ died for no purpose. - Galatians
2:20-21 ESV

Paul told the Galatians that this new life was the life of Christ in Him – "It is no longer I who live, but Christ who lives in me." Paul wanted to cultivate this new life. He desired to walk in the power and victory of this new life of Christ.

Paul attributed all his success in ministry to the work of the Lord Jesus in Him. He took no credit for this himself. Speaking to the Corinthians, he told them that the only boasting a believer could do was in the Lord and in what He had done and was doing through them:

(30) And because of him you are in Christ
Jesus, who became to us wisdom from
God, righteousness and sanctification and
redemption, (31) so that, as it is written,
"Let the one who boasts, boast in the
Lord." - 1 Corinthians 1:30-31 ESV

The righteousness God requires does not come from our sinful flesh. It is the work of His Son in, for and through us. The apostle Paul's prayer for the Philippians was that they would be filled with the fruit of righteousness that "comes through Jesus Christ, to the glory and praise of God:"

(9) And it is my prayer that your love may
abound more and more, with knowledge
and all discernment, (10) so that you may
approve what is excellent, and so be pure
and blameless for the day of Christ, (11)

filled with the fruit of righteousness that comes through Jesus Christ, to the glory and praise of God. - Philippians 1:9-11 ESV

Paul's prayer for himself was that He would gain Christ and experience the righteousness that comes through faith in Him:

(8) Indeed, I count everything as loss because of the surpassing worth of knowing Christ Jesus my Lord. For his sake I have suffered the loss of all things and count them as rubbish, in order that I may gain Christ (9) and be found in him, not having a righteousness of my own that comes from the law, but that which comes through faith in Christ, the righteousness from God that depends on faith— - Philippians 3:8-9 ESV

The apostle Peter introduced his second epistle with the following words:

(1) Simeon Peter, a servant and apostle of Jesus Christ, To those who have obtained a faith of equal standing with ours by the righteousness of our God and Savior Jesus Christ: - 2 Peter 1:1 ESV

Notice that the righteousness that comes by faith is the "righteousness of our God and Saviour Jesus Christ." In other words, it is not our ability to be right with God that counts, but the ability of Christ who lives in us to be right with God. The presence of Christ and His life and work in us gives us right standing with God. Our flesh and body will perish because of sin, but we have new life in Christ. Our old nature and body have been condemned to die. Though this dead body lingers with us, we have a new life and standing with the Father. We must now live in this new life. It is His presence that gives us right standing with the Father. Jesus not only makes us righteous, but He is also our righteousness. Without Him and His presence, we would never have a right standing with the Father.

For Prayer:

Father, I confess that I cannot please You in my flesh. I recognize that apart from Jesus Christ, I would be lost and under Your eternal judgement. I acknowledge that there is nothing good in my flesh. I also recognize that my sinful flesh and body are condemned because of sin. I praise you, however, that by faith in Jesus and His finished work, I have been born again into a new life. The life I have received through this new birth is the life of Christ in me. Thank you that I can now be restored to You and in a right relationship with You through the work of Jesus in me.

Lord Jesus, thank you for giving me new life and standing with the Father. Forgive me for still catering to the sinful, dying flesh. Forgive me for the many times I have looked to this sinful flesh and its wisdom. Teach me what it means to die to my old nature and live in You.

Chapter 8 – Christ Our Strength

In this final reflection, I want to consider the strength we have to live the Christian life. Consider the teaching of the apostle Paul in Philippians 4:

> *(12) I know how to be brought low, and I know how to abound. In any and every circumstance, I have learned the secret of facing plenty and hunger, abundance and need. (13) I can do all things through him who strengthens me. - Philippians 4:12-13 ESV*

Of all the apostles, Paul likely struggled the most. Speaking to Ananias, the Lord said about him:

> *(16) For I will show him how much he must suffer for the sake of my name." - Acts 9:16 ESV*

Paul told the Philippians that he knew what it was like to be brought low and face hunger and need. Where did he find the strength to endure such difficulties? He tells us in Philippians 4:13 that he could face these trials through the one who strengthened him. Paul found his strength to face the obstacles in this pathway through a person. That person was the Lord Jesus.

In the person of the Lord Jesus Christ, Paul found strength. He told the Corinthians that he was not sufficient in himself to do the task he had been called to do. His sufficiency, however, came through Christ. In the Lord Jesus, Paul had great confidence as a minister of the new covenant:

(4) Such is the confidence that we have through Christ toward God. (5) Not that we are sufficient in ourselves to claim anything as coming from us, but our sufficiency is from God, (6) who has made us sufficient to be ministers of a new covenant, not of the letter but of the Spirit. For the letter kills, but the Spirit gives life. - 2 Corinthians 3:4-6 ESV

In fact, it was the decision of Paul not to minister in his own wisdom and strength. Instead he determined to know and trust nothing but the person of Christ and the power of His Spirit as He worked among the Corinthians:

(2) For I decided to know nothing among you except Jesus Christ and him crucified. (3) And I was with you in weakness and in fear and much trembling, (4) and my speech and my message were not in plausible words of wisdom, but in demonstration of the Spirit and of power, (5) so that your faith might not rest in the wisdom of men but in the power of God. - 1 Corinthians 2:2-5 ESV

It was the desire of Paul to demonstrate the mighty power of Jesus Christ among the Corinthians so that their faith would not be in him as an apostle but in the Lord Jesus who worked through Him and in their midst.

All to much work is done in human strength and wisdom. When the wisdom and strength for the task can be traced back to individuals, the glory goes to them. When the power and wisdom can only be traced to God, however, He alone receives the glory. In the writing ministry God has given me, I have seen Him open doors to translate books in languages I never knew existed. I look back in wonder at how He has provided finances in ways I could never have imagined. I remember receiving and email from a Christian pastor who purchased my books from a Buddhist bookseller in Myanmar on the corner near his home. I have an envelope on my wall from a believer in India. The only correct information on the address is the ministry, street name and the country. I have no idea how this request for literature reached me with so little information but God saw fit for it to arrive. I keep that envelope on my wall as a reminder of the power of God to do what seems impossible.

For some people it is hard to imagine anything happening if they do not do it themselves. Paul told the Corinthians that he worked harder than any of them for the cause of Christ. Notice, however, how he qualifies this statement in 1 Corinthians 15:10:

> *(10) But by the grace of God I am what I am, and his grace toward me was not in vain. On the contrary, I worked harder than any of them, though it was not I, but the grace of God that is with me. - 1 Corinthians 15:10 ESV*

"I worked harder,... though it was not I, but the grace of God that was with me," Paul said. Yes, it was the voice of Paul that spoke. He was physically present among the Corinthians and at the end of the day his body was tired. Paul, however, had an awareness of the "grace" of God with Him. That grace came in the form of a calling and an equipping but it was more than that. The grace Paul speaks of here was the very presence of Christ in His ministry. That presence opened doors and accomplished what could never be achieved in Paul's own wisdom and strength.

Paul told the Colossians that he struggled with Christ's energy that was being powerfully worked in him:

> *(28) Him we proclaim, warning everyone and teaching everyone with all wisdom, that we may present everyone mature in Christ. (29) For this I toil, struggling with all his energy that he powerfully works within me.- Colossians 1:28-29 ESV*

Paul boldly proclaims here that the energy and strength of Christ was working powerfully in Him. He does not attribute any success to himself. Yes, he worked hard but the results and the enabling were not of His own making. It was the power of Jesus Christ in Him that kept Him going. It was the mighty work of God through Him that broke down the strongholds of Satan.

As the apostle looked over the great successes of ministry, he told the Corinthians that it was the miraculous power of God that produced the growth they had seen in their lives:

> *(6) I planted, Apollos watered, but God gave the growth. (7) So neither he who plants nor he who waters is anything, but only God who gives the growth. - 1 Corinthians 3:6-7 ESV*

I do not have the power of life in me. I cannot make a garden grow. The power of life is in God. He uses us to bring life to men and women around us, but the power is not in me but in Him alone.

Paul lived his life with the awareness of the power of Jesus in Him. He often saw himself unworthy of this but never took it for granted nor did he have any sense that this power was naturally in Him. He reminded the Ephesians that he was given the privilege to minister through God's grace and the working of Christ's power:

> *(7) Of this gospel I was made a minister according to the gift of God's grace, which was given me by the working of his power.*
> *- Ephesians 3:7 ESV*

The apostle did not believe that he alone was given this power from God. He reminded the Philippians that God was at work in them also:

> *(12) Therefore, my beloved, as you have always obeyed, so now, not only as in my presence but much more in my absence, work out your own salvation with fear and trembling, (13) for it is God who works in you, both to will and to work for his good pleasure. - Philippians 2:12-13 ESV*

God, according to the apostle was working in the Philippians to accomplish His purpose. All too often we fail to grasp the significance of this verse. The phrase, "it is God who works in you," is a very important. We are not left to do the work of maturing and serving God on our own. God is working in us to accomplish "His good pleasure." How important it is for us to recognize and submit to this work of God in our lives.

Listen to what Paul told the Ephesians

> *(20) Now to him who is able to do far more abundantly than all that we ask or think, according to the power at work*

within us, (21) to him be glory in the
church and in Christ Jesus throughout all
generations, forever and ever. Amen. -
Ephesians 3:20-21 ESV

According to Paul, God was able to do more than we could ever ask or think. Have you ever seen God break that hardened heart of a friend or loved one? Have you ever seen God do something in your life that leaves you speechless? Paul tells us that there is a power at work within us that can do things we never imagined. That power is the very life of Jesus working in us breaking down strongholds and giving life to what was once dead in us.

When He was on this earth, the Lord Jesus taught that our strength as believers was to be in Him. He reminds us to abide in Him and draw from His enabling. The apostle John records these words of Jesus:

(4) Abide in me, and I in you. As the
branch cannot bear fruit by itself, unless it
abides in the vine, neither can you, unless
you abide in me. (5) I am the vine; you
are the branches. Whoever abides in me
and I in him, he it is that bears much fruit,
for apart from me you can do nothing. -
John 15:4-5 ESV

What is impossible in our own strength and wisdom is more than possible in the strength of Jesus Christ who lives in us.

Jesus went on to tell us that while we will suffer in this world we are not to be anxious about what we are to say, because in the hour of our need, His Spirit would give us the words we need to speak. He would speak through us:

Christ Our Strength

(19) When they deliver you over, do not be anxious how you are to speak or what you are to say, for what you are to say will be given to you in that hour. (20) For it is not you who speak, but the Spirit of your Father speaking through you. - Matthew 10:19-20 ESV

Can you imagine this reality? The very words of God given to us to speak to our accusers. This is the promise of the Lord Jesus to those who know Him.

As believers we know that God gives us spiritual gifts for the service of the church. It is important for us to understand , however, that these gifts must be empowered by the person of God if they are to be effective.

(4) Now there are varieties of gifts, but the same Spirit; (5) and there are varieties of service, but the same Lord; (6) and there are varieties of activities, but it is the same God who empowers them all in everyone. - 1 Corinthians 12:4-6 ESV

This means that we cannot trust our spiritual gifts because the power does not come them but from the person of the Lord who chooses to empowers them.

Paul challenges us, therefore, to be strong in the person of the Lord and His strength.

(10) Finally, be strong in the Lord and in the strength of his might. - Ephesians 6:10 ESV

Where does the strength come from to overcome the temptations before us? The apostle Paul told the Corinthians that God Himself would provide the way for them to endure.

> *(13) No temptation has overtaken you that is not common to man. God is faithful, and he will not let you be tempted beyond your ability, but with the temptation he will also provide the way of escape, that you may be able to endure it. - 1 Corinthians 10:13 ESV*

The strength we need is found at the throne of Jesus who sympathizes with each us in our weakness. He provides all the grace we need to overcome.

> *(15) For we do not have a high priest who is unable to sympathize with our weaknesses, but one who in every respect has been tempted as we are, yet without sin. (16) Let us then with confidence draw to the throne of grace, that we may receive mercy and find grace to help in time of need. - Hebrews 4:15-16 ESV*

For those who want to serve the Lord but feel their weakness, the writer to the Hebrews tells us that the great shepherd of the sheep, Jesus Christ will equip us with every good thing we need to do what is pleasing to Him.

> *(20) Now may the God of peace who brought again from the dead our Lord Jesus, the great shepherd of the sheep, by the blood of the eternal covenant, (21) equip you with everything good that you may do his will, working in us that which is pleasing in his sight, through Jesus Christ,*

Christ Our Strength
to whom be glory forever and ever. Amen.
- Hebrews 13:20-21 ESV

What is the source of our strength? It is evident in Scripture that Jesus Himself is our strength. It is His power alone that can overcome the enemy. The apostles made a conscious decision not to trust their own strength but to walk in the strength of the Lord. This gave them great boldness in service. Jesus taught that we needed to abide in Him if we were going to bear any fruit. Our strength to do the task God has given us to do is not in ourselves but in Christ.

What I am trying to convey in this chapter is that the Lord Jesus is the strength we need. Once again, the strength I need to live the Christian life and serve God is not some impersonal force but in the person of the Lord Jesus. Apart from Him, we can do nothing of eternal significance.

For Prayer:

Father, I recognize that we often trust yourselves and our natural wisdom and ability in ministry. Thank you for the commitment of the apostle Paul to know nothing but Jesus and His power working in him so that all glory would go to God. Teach us Lord that Your presence in us is strength. Show us that apart from You and Your presence in us we have nothing of any eternal value to offer this world. I ask Lord that You would show us that difference between trying to live the Christian life in our own strength and being an instrument in the hands of the Lord Jesus to accomplish Your purpose in this world. Thank You Lord Jesus that I have this incredible privilege of being the one You use to advance Your kingdom. Teach me to know You and Your presence in my life. Teach me to discern Your purpose so that I can walk in harmony with You. May I trust what You are doing more than my own fleshly wisdom and strength. Thank you that You are my strength.

Chapter 9 – Final Word

I am sure there is much more to be said on this topic but I believe the point is made. In this final chapter, let me summarize what we have seen and emphasize the point of this study.

The Lord Jesus did more than save us –He is our salvation. We cannot separate salvation from the person of Jesus. We often speak of our salvation as something that happened to us. It is true that something wonderful did happen to us when we came to Christ. But that it just the point we are making in this study. We came to the person of Christ and were transformed. It was a person who made this change. It was an encounter with the Saviour that made the difference.

The apostle Paul persecuted believers and rejected their message of salvation apart from the Jewish law, but he was changed and became one of Christianity's greatest ambassadors. What made the difference? Paul's life was turned upside down when He met the Lord Jesus. He could never be the same after that encounter with Jesus on the road to Damascus.

The opening chapters of the Bible show us that the idea of saving humankind was God plan from the very beginning. In Genesis 3:15 He promised that the offspring of Eve would crush the head of the serpent. In other words, God would send His Son Jesus to this earth to deal with sin and the power of Satan over our hearts and lives. John describes

Jesus as the Word that would bring the light of life to His people (John 1:1-5). The apostle Peter tells us that the Lamb without blemish was foreknown before the foundation of the earth (1 Peter 1:19-20). Before the foundation of the earth was ever laid and human beings began to populate its surface, the Lord Jesus, the Lamb without blemish was waiting for the moment to reveal His salvation to the earth.

When the Lord Jesus did reveal Himself on this earth, He became the payment for our sin. He sacrificed Himself on the cross of Calvary to cover our debt. Our penalty was not paid with money, land or earthly treasures but by the death of the Lord Jesus, the Lamb of God. His very life is payment for sin. This means than that our forgiveness is in the person of the Lord Jesus. You cannot find forgiveness in anything you do or say. It can only be found in Him who bore our sins on the cross. Only those who enter the shelter of His loving arms can know this forgiveness. He is our forgiveness.

If we are to find the way to God, we must enter the right door. Jesus declares that He alone is the door (John 10:7-9). The shepherds of Bible times stood at the entrance to the sheep fold watching what came in and out. Nothing could enter unless they passed through them. Like these shepherds, the Lord Jesus is the doorway to heaven and eternal life. The way to heaven is found in the person of Jesus Christ. You may know the doctrine of salvation but until you stand before the person of Jesus Christ that doctrine will not save you. You must come to Jesus as the door if you are to enter into eternal life.

The truth upon which we base our lives as believers is found in the person of the Lord Jesus. The Scriptures of the Old Testament point to Him. The Gospels share with us His teaching and life. The writers of the New Testament all point us to Jesus and His work as the truth. What is truth? Jesus is truth. All He spoke and demonstrated by His life is the truth upon which our entire life is built.

Prior to knowing the Lord Jesus, we were dead to all things spiritual. When we met Jesus, something miraculous took place. We experienced a spiritual birth. We became new people. What took place that day? We experienced the life of Christ in us. Paul told the Colossians that Christ was their life (Colossians 3:4). Writing to the Galatians he said: "It is no longer I who live, but Christ who lives in me" (Galatians 2:20). This new life we experience is the life of Jesus Christ in us. What an incredible privilege it is to have His presence in us to empower and strengthen us in the task before us. We indeed have a treasure in a jar of clay (2 Corinthians 4:7).

Because of the presence of the Lord Jesus in us and only because of Him can we have a right standing with the Father. Everyone of us has fallen short of the standard of God. Jesus is the payment for our sin. To be in Christ is to be in a right standing with God for His righteousness covers us. Apart from Christ, however, there is no standing with God at all. Jesus is our right standing with the Father. He alone has measured up to the standard. I stand in Him if I am to stand before the Father.

Everything I need to live the Christian life is in Jesus and His presence in me. How easy it is to try with all out might and wisdom to serve the Lord. The strength and wisdom to do this is not in me. For many years I wrestled with the frustration of trying to serve the Lord in my own strength. I am coming to realize that it is not so much what I do for God as it is what He does through me that counts. My desire is to merely be an instrument through which Christ can work. My role is to be obedient and submissive to what He wants to do. I am not

73

in charge –He is. When I stand before God, I will not say to Him, "look at all the things I did for You." Instead, I will bow down before Him in praise for all the things He has done through undeserving me. You see, Jesus is the strength in me. It is He who works in me. Yes, I need to be obedient but I am His servant. I come to the end of the day with a tired body but I am aware that the wisdom and power behind my physical, emotional and spiritual efforts is not mine but His. My strength and wisdom is in the person of the Lord Jesus.

How easy it is to make salvation all about a doctrine or lifestyle and not about the person of Christ. We can make the Christian life all about our efforts and practices and not about the indwelling presence of Jesus. Salvation is about a person. The focus of our life needs to be upon the person of Jesus Christ and His work in us. I have met all too many Christians who have lost their focus. Their hearts have become distracted and they have lost sight of Christ. May God give us the grace to see that our salvation and Christian life from start to finish is about the person of the Lord Jesus. May we never lose sight of Him and His work in our lives.

For Prayer:

Lord Jesus, forgive me for the times that I have lost sight of You in my life. Forgive me for the times I have made my faith more about my efforts than about Your work in me. I confess that I have often forged ahead of You in service. I have loved my traditions and doctrines more than I have loved You. Thank you, Lord, that You are my salvation and forgiveness. Thank you for Your life in me that empowers me, forgives me and gives me a right standing with the Father. I confess that apart from You I would be eternally lost. I confess that the flesh cannot please You or truly accomplish Your purpose. May my greatest desire be to know You Lord and be an instrument in Your hands.

Light To My Path Book Distribution

Light To My Path Book Distribution (LTMP) is a book writing and distribution ministry reaching out to needy Christian workers in Asia, Latin America, and Africa. Many Christian workers in developing countries do not have the resources necessary to obtain Bible training or purchase Bible study materials for their ministries and personal encouragement.

F. Wayne Mac Leod is a member of Action International Ministries and has been writing these books with a goal to distribute them freely to needy pastors and Christian workers around the world.

These books are being used in preaching, teaching, evangelism and encouragement of local believers in over sixty countries. Books have now been translated into several languages. The goal is to make them available to as many believers as possible.

The ministry of LTMP is a faith-based ministry, and we trust the Lord for the resources necessary to distribute the books for the encouragement and strengthening of believers around the world. Would you pray that the Lord would open doors for the translation and further distribution of these books? For more information about Light To My Path Book Distribution visit our website at https://www.lighttomypath.ca

Printed in Great Britain
by Amazon

85542943R00047